W9-ATT-500

LEVEL
1

Polar Bears

Laura Marsh

▢ NATIONAL
GEOGRAPHIC

Washington, D.C.

For Eva —L.F.M.

The publisher and author gratefully acknowledge the expert
assistance of Geoff York of WWF Canada.

Book design by YAY! Design

Paperback ISBN: 978-1-4263-1104-8
Library ISBN: 978-1-4263-1105-5

Photo credits

Cover, Klein-Hubert/Kimball Stock; 1, Judith Conning/National Geographic My Shot; 2, Steven Kazlowski /naturepl.
com; 4, Ralph Lee Hopkins/National Geographic Creative/Getty Images; 6, Hemis/Alamy; 7, Siddhardha Gargie/
National Geographic My Shot; 8, Steven Kazlowski /naturepl.com; 9, Steven Kazlowski/naturepl.com; 10, Michael
Weber/SuperStock; 12, ZSSD/Minden Pictures/Corbis; 14, SuperStock; 15, Flip Nicklin/National Geographic Stock; 16,
Alaska Stock/Corbis; 16-17, Richard Ress/National Geographic My Shot; 18, Matthias Breiter/Minden Pictures; 20, Rolf
Hicker Photography/Alamy; 22 (UP), gary718/Shutterstock; 22 (CTR), Matt Propert/National Geographic Stock; 22 (LO),
Christopher Drake/National Geographic My Shot; 23 (UPLE), EcoStock/Shutterstock; 23 (UPRT), Flip Nicklin/Minden
Pictures; 23 (LOLE), primopiano/Shutterstock; 23 (LORT), John Conrad/Corbis; 24, Jenny E. Ross/Corbis; 25, Matthias
Breiter/Minden Pictures; 26, T.J. Rich/naturepl.com; 28 (UP), Daniel J Cox/Getty Images; 28 (LO), AFP/Getty Images; 29,
Linda Drake/National Geographic My Shot; 30 (LE), Keith Levit Photography RF/Getty Images; 30 (RT), Valerie Abbott/
National Geographic My Shot; 31 (UPLE), Sergey Rusakov/Shutterstock; 31 (UPRT), Matt Propert/National Geographic
Stock; 31 (LOLE), Pradeep Chitta/National Geographic My Shot; 31 (LORT), Vladimir Melnik/Shutterstock; 32 (UPLE),
Fedorov Oleksiy/Shutterstock; 32 (UPRT), Flip Nicklin/National Geographic Stock; 32 (LOLE), Andy Barnes/National
Geographic My Shot; 32 (LORT), Uryadnikov Sergey/Shutterstock; header, Nebojsa S/Shutterstock

Table of Contents

Who Am I?

I'm white and
furry, and I
swim in the sea.

The cold snow
and ice are just
right for me.

Who am I?
A polar bear!

Big Bears!

Have you seen a polar bear in a zoo?
Polar bears are big—really big.

They are the biggest meat-eaters
on land. A polar bear can weigh as
much as seven men!

A polar bear's body is built for the Arctic. These bears have thick fur to keep them warm.

Polar bears have thick fat, too. The fat keeps body heat in and keeps the Arctic cold out.

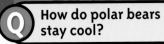

Q How do polar bears stay cool?

A They turn on bear conditioning!

Word Bite

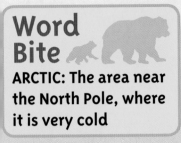

ARCTIC: The area near the North Pole, where it is very cold

9

Powerful Paws

Long, thick, curved claws grab food easily.

Thick pads keep feet warm.

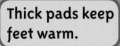

Front paws are webbed, like ducks' feet. This helps polar bears swim.

Bumps on the footpads keep bears from slipping on the ice.

A polar bear's paws do many things. Paws dig dens in the snow. They break the ice to find food. They also pull food out of the water.

Big paws keep bears from sinking into the snow. The paws are larger than a dinner plate!

Word Bite

DEN: A hidden hole where a wild animal lives. Polar bear mothers have their babies in a den.

Super Swimmers

Polar bears are great swimmers. They spend a lot of time in the water.

Their front paws paddle.
Their back legs steer. Their fat
helps polar bears float.

Word Bite

FLOAT: To rest or move in
water without sinking

What's for Dinner?

A polar bear eats other animals.
Seals are its favorite food.
This bear is hunting seals on
the sea ice.

Seals come up for air at holes in the ice. The bear waits and waits. Finally, a seal appears. The polar bear snatches it in a flash.

Polar bears have good noses. They can smell a seal 20 miles away!

Polar bears have good hearing and eyesight, too. These come in handy when looking for dinner. This bear has spotted an arctic fox.

The ice melts in spring and summer. Polar bears stay with the ice when they can. They move to land when the sea ice is mostly gone.

On land they usually don't eat at all. Some bears may eat bird eggs. They may eat plants or berries. But there is not much food for polar bears on land.

19

Bears in Town

In Churchill, Canada, polar bears come to town in the fall! The ice is melting earlier each year. It is forming later, too. The bears are hungry. They are looking for food.

Our Earth is getting warmer. There is less sea ice now. This is dangerous for polar bears. They need the ice to hunt.

21

7 Amazing Polar Bear Facts

1

The largest polar bear ever recorded was 2,209 pounds. That's the weight of a small sports car!

2

Polar bears have black skin underneath their white fur.

3

Sometimes polar bears get too hot. Then they take a swim or roll in the snow.

4

Walruses are one of the few animals that polar bears are afraid of.

5

Some people go on vacations to see polar bears. They ride in special buggies to stay safe.

6

Polar bears can eat 100 pounds of seal fat at one time. That's about as heavy as 400 hamburgers!

7

Polar bears clean themselves by rubbing their bodies on the snow.

Cute Cubs

Every new polar bear is special.
A mother bear has babies, called
cubs. She digs a den in the snow.
The cubs stay safe and warm in
the den.

Word Bite

CUB: A baby bear

The cubs drink their mother's rich milk. They grow quickly. Soon they are big enough to leave the den.

A mother polar bear teaches her cubs to hunt. She also teaches them how to stay safe and warm.

The cubs leave their mother when they are two years old. They are ready to live on their own.

27

Playtime!

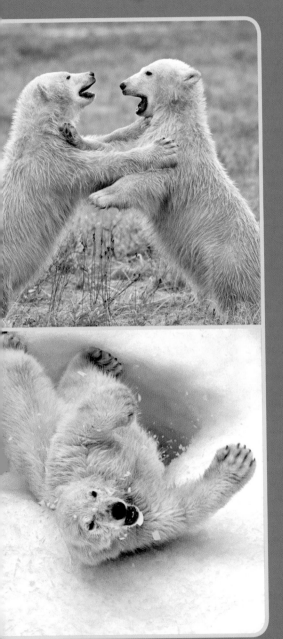

Polar bears
like to play just
like you!

Bears wrestle
with each other.
They slide
in the snow.
They like to
play games, too.

Sometimes a cub gets a ride from Mom! These bears are off on an Arctic adventure.

What in the World?

These pictures show up-close views of things in a polar bear's world. Use the hints to figure out what's in the pictures. Answers are on page 31.

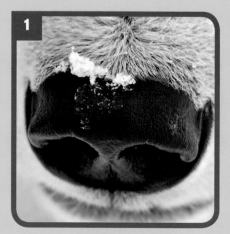

HINT: Helps find dinner

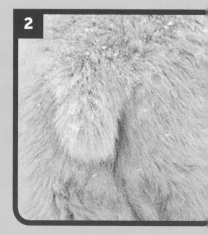

HINT: You don't have one of these.

HINT: A polar bear's favorite food

HINT: Keeps a bear warm

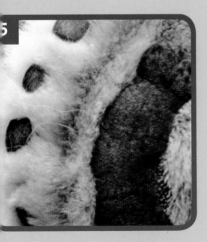

HINT: Built for snow, ice, and water

HINT: Polar bears are afraid of this animal.

Answers: 1. Nose, 2. Tail, 3. Seal, 4. Fur, 5. Paw, 6. Walr...

31

ARCTIC: The area near the North Pole, where it is very cold

CUB: A baby bear

DEN: A hidden hole where a wild animal lives. Polar bear mothers have their babies in a den.

FLOAT: To rest or move in water without sinking

Monkeys

Anne Schreiber

NATIONAL
GEOGRAPHIC

Washington, D.C.

To Jacob, Sammy, and Noah—a barrel of monkeys!
—A. S.

The publisher and author gratefully acknowledge the review
of proofs for this book by Joe Knobbe of the Saint Louis Zoo and
Keith Lovett of the Palm Beach Zoo.

ISBN: 978-1-4263-1106-2 (Trade paper)
ISBN: 978-1-4263-1107-9 (Library)

Design by YAY! Design

Photo Credits
Cover, Elio Della Ferrera/naturepl.com; 1, Josh Brown/National Geographic My Shot; 2, Imagewerks Japan/Getty Images; 4-5
Brad Starry/National Geographic My Shot; 7 (UPLE), Pete Oxford/Minden Pictures; 7 (UPRT), Fiona Rogers/naturepl.com; 7 (LO
Chiangkunta/Flickr RM/Getty Images; 8, Thomas Marent/Minden Pictures/Corbis; 9, Danita Delimont/Alamy; 10-11, Marsel va
Oosten/www.squiver.com; 13 (UPLE), Thomas Marent/Visuals Unlimited, Inc./Getty Images; 13 (UPRT), Judith Arsenault/Natio
Geographic My Shot; 13 (LE CTR), Anup Shah/Corbis; 13 (RT CTR), Jennifer Kraft/National Geographic My Shot; 13 (LOLE), Dr. Cliv
Bromhall/Getty Images; 13 (LORT), Judith Arsenault/National Geographic My Shot; 14, Jerry Young/Dorling Kindersley; 15, Eri
Isselée/Shutterstock; 16, Christianne Lagura/National Geographic Stock; 17, Thomas Marent/Minden Pictures/Corbis; 18, Don
Tramontozzi/National Geographic My Shot; 19, Bruno D'Amicis/naturepl.com; 20, Pete Oxford/Minden Pictures/Corbis; 22, S
Team/Foto Natura/Minden Pictures; 23, Pornchai Kittiwongsakul/AFP/Getty Images; 24 (UP), Mario Tizon/National Geograph
My Shot; 24 (CTR), Cathleen Burnham/National Geographic My Shot; 24 (LO), AP Photo/Public Library of Science, Maurice
Emetshu; 25 (UP), Anup Shah/Getty Images; 25 (CTR), Frank Lukasseck/Getty Images; 25 (LO), Mint Images-Frans Lanting/Get
Images; 26-27, Cyril Ruoso/JH Editorial/Minden Pictures/Corbis; 28, Mattias Klum/National Geographic Stock; 29, Barbara
Walton/epa/Corbis; 30 (UP), Karl Ammann/Digital Vision; 30 (CTR), Matt Propert/National Geographic Society; 30 (LO), Jerem
Phan/National Geographic My Shot; 31 (UPLE), James Pelton/National Geographic My Shot; 31 (UPRT), Branislav Bieleny/Natior
Geographic My Shot; 31 (LE CTR), M Rutherford/Shutterstock; 31 (RT CTR), Sebastien Barreau/National Geographic My Shot; 3
(LOLE), Andrey Pavlov/Shutterstock; 31 (LORT), Hakuei Huang/National Geographic My Shot; 32 (UPLE), Anna Kucherova/Shut
terstock; 32 (UPRT), Jeff Mauritzen/Shutterstock; 32 (LE CTR), Cyril Ruoso/JH Editorial/Minden Pictures/Corbis; 32 (RT CTR), Galyna Andrushke
Shutterstock; 32 (LOLE), worldswildlifewonders/Shutterstock; 32 (LORT), Dr. Clive Bromhall/Getty Images; art in running head
stock09/Shutterstock; art in "Monkey Talk" boxes, Brad Collett/Shutterstock.

Table of Contents

Monkey Business

Yellow baboons

Who spends their
days climbing in trees,
leaping up high or
swinging with ease?

Who calls out in
grunts, screeches,
or whoops?

Who lives together in
groups we call troops?

Monkeys, that's who!

Monkeying Around

Monkeys live in many different kinds of habitats. They live in jungles and on mountains. They live in rain forests, grasslands, and even in cities and towns.

Many monkeys are arboreal (ar–BOR–ee–ul) monkeys. That means they live in the trees. Other monkeys live mostly on the ground.

Monkey Talk

HABITAT: The place where a plant or animal lives in nature

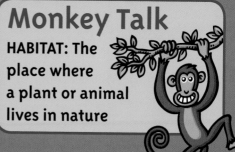

Gelada baboon

Common marmoset

Macaque

Monkey Talk

CANOPY: The area high up in the trees

PREHENSILE: Made for grabbing hold, like some monkeys' tails

The spider monkey uses its strong, prehensile (pree-HEN-sil) tail to grab and hold on.

Life in the Trees

Many arboreal monkeys live in the canopy (KAN-uh-pee) layer of the trees. They move from branch to branch.

Why don't they fall? Some monkeys use their tails like a third arm. Other monkeys have pads on their bottoms to keep them in place.

A colobus monkey using its bottom pads to stay put

Ah, the Spa!

Snow monkeys are macaques (muh-KAKS). Many of them live in the mountains of Japan. These monkeys know how to warm up in the winter.

Snow monkeys

They bathe in the hot mountain water. The water is heated inside the Earth and bubbles to the surface. Snow monkeys like to relax and play in the warm water.

All in the Family

Monkeys and apes are both primates (PRY-mates). Primates are animals known for their big brains. They are smart. Their eyes face straight ahead. Sound like someone you know?

Surprise! Humans are primates, too. Humans are in the ape family! Chimpanzees, bonobos, orangutans, gibbons, gorillas, and humans are all apes.

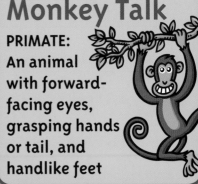

Monkey Talk

PRIMATE: An animal with forward-facing eyes, grasping hands or tail, and handlike feet

Apes	Monkeys

TAIL

do not have tails	have tails

BODY

...ally larger, can walk on two legs	usually smaller, walk on four legs

BRAIN

...very smart, most use tools	smart, most do not use tools

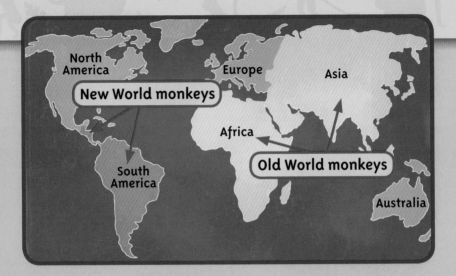

New World monkeys live in parts of Central and South America. They are small and have flat noses. They live in trees.

Capuchin monkeys live in part of Central and South America.

Old World monkeys live in parts of Africa and Asia. They are larger, and their noses are not flat. They live in mountains, grasslands, forests, and towns. They sit on their bottom pads.

Vervet monkeys live in parts of Africa.

Monkey Babies

Monkey mothers have a strong bond with their babies. This bond helps babies learn from their mothers. Monkey babies stay close to their moms for the first year.

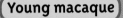

Young macaque

16

Silvered leaf monkeys

A newborn monkey holds on tight to its mother's front. Later, it rides on its mom's back.

Baboons

Barbary macaques

Young monkeys play together. They wrestle and tumble. When boys are older, they usually go off to join another troop. Most girl monkeys stay with their moms. One day they will raise their own families.

Tools of the Trade

Brown capuchin

Q What do you get when you cross a jungle with an office?

A Monkey business.

Most monkeys don't use tools. But capuchin (KA-pyu-shen) monkeys do! They sometimes use tools to find food. They use rocks to dig up potatoes. They also use rocks to crack open nuts and seeds.

Rocks aren't the only tools these monkeys use. When capuchin monkeys need to protect themselves against snakes, they may use a tree branch as a club.

Want a Banana?

Do you have to eat your fruits and vegetables? Monkeys do, too!

Monkeys eat more than 200 different types of food.

Most monkeys eat plants such as seed, leaves, and fruit, including bananas! Monkeys sometimes eat insects, too.

This Midas tamarin is eating seed pods.

Every year people in the city of Lopburi, Thailand, throw a party for the macaque monkeys that live there. People put out more than 4,000 pounds of food for the monkeys!

6 Marvelous Monkeys

Loudest!

Howler monkeys can be heard up to three miles away.

Tiniest!

The pygmy marmoset is the world's smallest monkey. It's about the size of a banana.

Newest Found!

The lesula monkey was just discovered in the Democratic Republic of the Congo in Africa.

Biggest!

A male mandrill can be three feet long. It weighs about 77 to 100 pounds. That's as big as a large dog.

Furriest!

Golden snub-nosed monkeys have thick fur to keep them warm. They live in the cold mountains of China.

Fastest!

Patas can run up to 35 miles an hour. That's as fast as a racehorse.

Friends and Family

Monkeys have strong bonds with the other members of their troop.

Grooming is the main way monkeys show they care. Mothers groom babies. Females groom other females. And couples groom each other.

Monkey Talk

GROOM: To clean, brush, and care for

Hanuman langurs

Monkeys in Trouble

What animal is the biggest danger to monkeys? Humans!

We have cut down forests where monkeys live. Without forests, monkeys have no place to go.

Forests that have been cut down in Malaysia

Proboscis (proh-BOS-is) monkeys live in the jungles of Borneo. Only a few thousand of them are left in the world. The mangrove forests they need for food are disappearing.

But some people are working to protect the land where monkeys live. This will help keep these amazing animals in our world.

Stump Your Parents

Can your parents answer these questions about monkeys? You might know more than they do!

Answers are at the bottom of page 31.

1

Where do monkeys live?

A. In cities
B. In forests
C. In jungles
D. All of the above

2

A monkey uses its prehensile tail to _____.

A. Fight
B. Sleep
C. Grab
D. Smell

Some monkeys are arboreal. Where do arboreal animals spend most of their time?

A. On the ground
B. In the air
C. In trees
D. Underwater

3

4

When a baby monkey is born, she _____.

A. Stays in her mother's pouch
B. Clings to her mother's front
C. Hangs from her mother's tail
D. Can immediately climb trees

5

Which animals are primates?

A. Monkeys
B. Great apes
C. Humans
D. All of the above

6

What do monkeys eat?

A. Bananas
B. Insects
C. Seeds
D. All of the above

7

What is the main way that monkeys show they care for each other?

A. They jump up and down.
B. They climb together.
C. They groom each other.
D. They play board games.

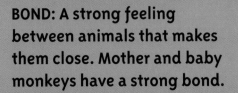

BOND: A strong feeling between animals that makes them close. Mother and baby monkeys have a strong bond.

CANOPY: The area high up in the trees

GROOM: To clean, brush, and care for

HABITAT: The place where a plant or animal lives in nature

PREHENSILE: Made for grabbing hold, like some monkeys' tails

PRIMATE: An animal with forward-facing eyes, grasping hands or tail, and handlike feet

Penguins

Anne Schreiber

NATIONAL GEOGRAPHIC

Washington, D.C.

To Hannah Sage and Hannah Rose
—A.S.

Copyright © 2009 National Geographic Society

Published by the National Geographic Society, Washington, D.C. 20036.

Library of Congress Cataloging-in-Publication Data
Schreiber, Anne.
Penguins! / Anne Schreiber.
p. cm.
ISBN 978-1-4263-0426-2 (pbk. : alk. paper) — ISBN 978-1-4263-0427-9
(library binding : alk. paper)
1. Penguins—Juvenile literature. I. Title.
QL696.S473S37 2009
598.47—dc22
2008022879

Cover: © Frans Lanting/Corbis; 1: © Marco Simoni/Robert Harding World Imagery/Getty Images; 2: © Bryan & Cherry Alexander/Seapics.com; 4-5: © Shutterstock; 8 (left), 32 (bottom, right): © Marc Chamberlain/Seapics.com; 6-7, 32 (top, right), 32 (middle, right): © Martin Walz; 8-9: © Bill Curtsinger/National Geographic/Getty Images; 8 (left inset), 14-15: © Seth Resnick/Science Faction/Getty Images; 8 (bottom inset): © Fritz Poelking/V&W/Seapics.com; 9 (top inset), 26 (top, left): © Shutterstock; 9 (right inset): © Worldfoto/Alamy; 10-11, 14 (inset), 32 (bottom, left): © Paul Nicklen/National Geographic/Getty Images; 12: © Jude Gibbons/Alamy; 13, 32 (top, left): © Martin Creasser/Alamy; 16, 32 (middle, left): © Colin Monteath/Hedgehog House/Getty Images; 17: © Kim Westerskov/Getty Images; 18: © Maria Stenzel/Corbis; 19: © blickwinkel/Lohmann/Alamy; 20, 22: © DLILLC/Corbis; 21: © Sue Flood/The Image Bank/Getty Images; 23: © Graham Robertson/Minden Pictures; 24-25: © Paul Souders/Photodisc/Getty Images; 26-29 (background): © Magenta/Alamy; 26 (top, center), 26 (bottom, right): © Tui de Roy/Minden Pictures; 26 (top, right): © Barry Bland/Nature Picture Library; 26 (bottom, left): © Kevin Schafer/Alamy; 27 (top, left), 29 (top, left): © W. Perry Conway/Corbis; 27 (top, right): © Rolf Hicker Photography/drr.net; 27 (bottom, left): © Sam Sarkis/Photographer's Choice/Getty Images; 27 (bottom, right): © Zach Holmes/Alamy; 28 (top, left): © Konrad Wothe/Minden Pictures/Getty Images; 28: (top, right): © Tom Brakefield/Photodisc/Getty Images; 28 (bottom, left): © Ingrid Visser/Seapics.com; 28 (bottom, right): © T.J. Rich/Nature Picture Library; 29 (top, right): © NaturephotoOnline/Alamy; 29 (bottom, left): © Photodisc/Alamy; 29 (bottom, right): © Bryan & Cherry Alexander/Alamy; 30: © Solvin Zankl/drr.net; 31 (top, left): © Andy Rouse/Corbis; 31 (bottom, left): © Darrell Gulin/Photographer's Choice/Getty Images; 31 (right): © David Tipling/The Image Bank/Getty Images; 32 (bottom, right): © Michael S. Nolan/Seapics.com

Table of Contents

What Are They?

EMPEROR PENGUINS

What birds cannot fly?
What birds spend most of their
lives in the ocean but are not fish?
What birds live in the coldest part
of the world — all year long?

They swim, they march, they
slide through the snow.

They are penguins.

Where Are They?

EQUATOR

SOUTH
AMERICA

BIRD WORDS

EQUATOR: An imaginary line halfway between the North and South Poles.

COAST: Where land meets water.

SOUTH P

All penguins live between the Equator and the South Pole. Some live where it's very cold. Some live in warmer places like the coasts of Africa or Australia.

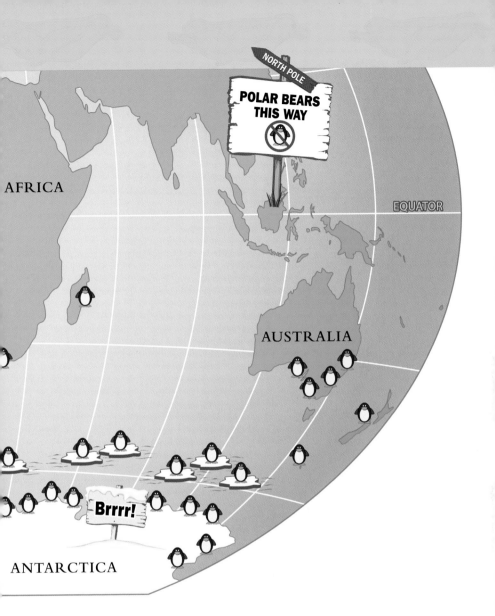

Penguins live on islands, on coasts, and even on icebergs in the sea. They just need to be near water, because they spend most of their lives IN the water.

Not Just Any Bird

EMPEROR PENGUIN

Big webbed feet for better steering.

Layers of soft feathers trap heat. Stiff, oily feathers on top keep out water.

Penguins are perfect for their lives at sea. They have a sleek shape for speed. A layer of blubber keeps them warm.

Stiff flippers act like boat paddles to push and steer.

Big eyes to see underwater.

BIRD WORDS

WEBBED: Connected by skin.

9

Their black backs make them hard to see from above. Their light bellies make them hard to see from below. But it's their strong, solid flippers that help them escape predators and get where they want to go.

Penguins can swim about 15 miles an hour. When they want to go faster, they leap out of the water as they swim. It's called porpoising (por-puh-sing), because it's what porpoises do.

GENTOO PENGUINS

A predator is an animal that eats other animals.

11

What's for Dinner?

HUMBOLT PENGUIN

Life in the ocean is fish-elicious! Penguins eat a lot of fish. They have a hooked bill, or beak, to help them grab their dinner. Barbs on their tongues and in their throats help them to hold on to slippery food.

Would you like a drink of salty water to go with that fish? Penguins are able to clean the salt out of ocean water. They get fresh water to drink and the salt dribbles back into the ocean.

BIRD WORDS

BARB: Something sharp and pointy like a hook.

13

MARINE MAMMALS: Have fur and give birth to live young; unlike other mammals, they spend most of their time in the ocean.

While penguins are slurping down their dinners, they have to be careful not to end up as dinner themselves. Penguins are the favorite food of marine mammals such as leopard seals and killer whales.

GENTOO PENGUINS AND A SKUA

Penguins are also in danger on land. Birds like the skua, the Australian sea eagle, and the giant petrel eat penguins. Even cats, snakes, foxes, and rats eat penguins when they can.

Life on Land

KING PENGUINS

BIRD WORDS

COLONY: A group of animals who live together.

On land, most penguins live in a large colony with thousands or even millions of other penguins. If it's cold, they huddle together. It's so warm inside a huddle that penguins take turns moving to the outside to cool off.

KING PENGUIN HUDDLE

Penguins march together to get to their nesting grounds. Once there they wave, strut, shake, call, nod, dance, and sing to find a mate. Most penguins stay with their mate for many years.

A Chick Is Born

CHINSTRAP CHICKS

Most penguins lay two eggs at a time, but often only one egg survives. The mother and father take turns keeping the egg warm. When it hatches, the parents keep the chick warm and fed.

ADELIE CHICKS

After a couple of weeks, hundreds or even thousands of chicks wait together while the parents go back to the sea to find food. As the chicks wait, they are in constant danger from skuas, eagles, and other animals.

KING CHICK

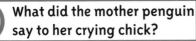

GENTOO FEEDING CHICK

Finally, the parents return with food. They have to find their chicks in a huge crowd of baby birds. How do they do it? The baby birds sing special songs to help their parents find them.

In a few months, the whole family returns to the sea.

The Longest March

EMPEROR PENGUINS

For the emperor penguins, getting to their nesting grounds is hard work. Their home is Antarctica—the coldest place on Earth.

Emperor penguins nest much farther from the ocean than other penguins. They must march for days and nights through snow and wind.

After laying her egg, the female gives it to the male. He will keep it warm in a flap under his belly. Unlike other penguins, the male emperor cares for the egg by himself while the female goes back to the ocean to find food.

The mother is gone for more than four months. The father huddles with the other male penguins to keep himself, and his egg, safe and warm. During this time, the father eats nothing but snow.

When the mother returns in July, the father quickly goes to the ocean to find food. By December, the whole family is ready to go.

Penguin Parade

Galapagos

HEIGHT
18"–21"

Fairy

HEIGHT
16"

SMALLEST

Fairy penguins sing more songs than any other penguins.

Snares

HEIGHT
21"–25"

Fiordland

HEIGHT
24"

Erect-Crested

HEIGHT
24"–26"

There are 17 different species,
or kinds, of penguins.

Rockhopper

HEIGHT
21"–25"

Yellow-Eyed

HEIGHT
23"–30"

These penguins are the loudest.
They sound like donkeys.

Magellanic

HEIGHT
24"–28"

African

HEIGHT
24"–28"

Macaroni

HEIGHT
21"–26"

Royal

HEIGHT
24"–28"

These penguins are the fastest swimmers.

Chinstrap

HEIGHT
27"

Gentoo

HEIGHT
27"–30"

Adelie
HEIGHT
22″–26″

Humboldt
HEIGHT
22″–26″

These penguins don't make a nest.
They carry their eggs wherever they go.

King
HEIGHT
37″

LARGEST
Emperor
HEIGHT
44″

Penguin Play

HOPPING: Rockhoppers can hop five feet high!

ROCKHOPPER PENGUIN

Life isn't always easy for penguins.
But at least they look like they're
having fun.

SINGING: Adults
sing to their mates,
and chicks sing for
their parents.

MACARONI PENGUIN

SLEDDING: Penguins speed
down icy hills on their feet and
bellies to get somewhere fast.

KING PENGUIN

SURFING: Penguins surf
through the waves.
Sometimes they surf right
from the water up onto land.

CHINSTRAP PENGUIN

31

BARB
Something sharp and pointy
like a hook.

COAST
Where land meets water.

COLONY
A group of animals who
live together.

EQUATOR
An imaginary line halfway between the North and South pol

MARINE MAMMALS
Have fur and give birth to live young;
unlike other mammals, they spend most
of their time in the ocean.

WEBBED
Connected by skin.

Saving Animal Babies

Amy Shields

NATIONAL
GEOGRAPHIC

Washington, D.C.

Thanks to all the people who love and care for animals,
especially Mary Fleming, Dr. Greg Mertz, Dr. Lori Perkins,
Justine Brewer, and Dr. Laurie Gage. —A. S.

The publisher and author gratefully acknowledge the expert assistance
of Ron Tilson of the Minnesota Zoo Foundation.

Design by YAY! Design

Paperback ISBN: 978-1-4263-1040-9
Library ISBN: 978-1-4263-1041-6

Photo Credits

Cover, Ron Kimball/www.kimballstock.com; 1, DLILLC/Corbis; 2, Peleg Elkalay/Shutterstock; 4-5, Erik Beiersmann/
dpa/Corbis; 7 (UP), Horst Ossinger/AFP/Getty Image; 7 (LO), Imaginechina/Corbis; 8, Smithsonian's National Zoo; 9,
Smithsonian's National Zoo; 11, Andrew Cunningham, Cummings School of Veterinary Medicine, Tufts University; 12,
Andrew Cunningham, Cummings School of Veterinary Medicine, Tufts University; 13, Southwick's Zoo and Belinda
Mazur; 15, Courtesy of Zoo Atlanta; 16, Courtesy of Zoo Atlanta; 17, Courtesy of Zoo Atlanta; 18 (UPLE), Vanderlei Almei-
da/AFP/GettyImages; 18 (UPRT), Suzi Eszterhas/Minden Pictures; 18 (LO), Martina Stevens, Houston Zoo; 19 (UP), John
MacDougall/AFP/Getty Images; 19 (CTR), Yu Qibo/Xinhua Press/Corbis; 19 (LO), Steven Good/Shutterstock; 20, Alex
Mustard/2020VISION/naturepl.com; 22, © National Aquarium; 23, © National Aquarium; 24, Dr. Greg Mertz; 25 (UP),
Dr. Greg Mertz; 25 (LO), Dr. Greg Mertz; 26, Dr. Greg Mertz; 27 (UP), Dr. Greg Mertz; 27 (LORT), Dr. Greg Mertz; 27 (LOLE),
Dr. Greg Mertz; 28 (UPRT), Sarah2/Shutterstock; 28 (UPLE), photomaster/Shutterstock; 28 (LO), v.s. anandhakrishna/
Shutterstock; 29 (UPLE), Vitali Burlakou/Shutterstock; 29 (UPRT), Dimj/Shutterstock; 29 (LE CTR), Diane Macdonald/
Getty Images; 29 (RT CTR), Picsfive/Shutterstock; 29 (LO), Marina Jay/Shutterstock; 30 (UP), Imaginechina/Corbis; 30
(LOLE), Ferry Indrawang/Shutterstock; 30 (LORT), Simon Greig/Shutterstock; 31 (UPLE), Derek R. Audette/Shutterstock;
31 (UPRT), Dougal Waters/Getty Images; 31 (LOLE), Ekkachai/Shutterstock; 31 (LORT), Mint Images RM/Getty Images; 32
(UPLE), Franco Tempesta; 32 (UPRT), Courtesy of Zoo Atlanta; 32 (LE CTR), Zurijeta/Shutterstock; 32 (RT CTR), Erik Beiers-
mann/dpa/Corbis; 32 (LOLE), Shutterstock; 32 (LORT), © National Aquarium; header, Potapov Alexander/Shutterstock;
vocabulary boxes, Vule/Shutterstock, nemlaza/Shutterstock.

Table of Contents

The Cubs Are Coming!

It is a dark and quiet night at the zoo. The tiger is restless. The zookeeper thinks the tiger will have her babies soon. And she does.

Tiger babies are called cubs.

There are four new tigers in the world! Tigers are in danger of becoming extinct. That means every tiger is special.

Wild Word
EXTINCT: A group of animals that is no longer living

Eat, Sleep, Repeat!

This is the tiger's first litter of cubs. Some tigers don't take care of their first litter. Without help, the cubs could die. But caretakers at the zoo know what to do.

At first, the cubs only need to eat and sleep. Every three hours, the cubs drink warm milk.

The cubs have a blanket that smells like their mother. Sleep well, little tigers.

Wild Word
LITTER: All the babies born to an animal at one time

Would you like to try a chunky meat milk shake? The cubs are crazy for them.

First the veterinarian checks the cubs' baby teeth. They need to be strong and sharp to chew the chunks. Then the zoo chef buys jars of turkey baby food. He mixes it with milk and vitamins to make the milk shake.

The vet sees that this cub's teeth are healthy.

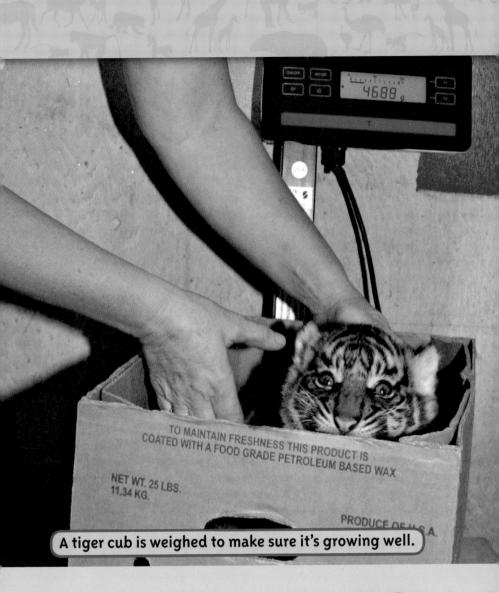

A tiger cub is weighed to make sure it's growing well.

Now the cubs will grow even faster. One day they will be full-grown tigers.

Wild Word
VETERINARIAN: A doctor for animals, called vet for short

A Long, Tall Baby

Molly is three days old. She is an 80-pound, 5-foot-tall baby giraffe. This baby should drink three gallons of milk a day. But her mother cannot make milk for her.

Molly also has an infection. She needs help. She has to go to the hospital.

Wild Word
INFECTION: A sickness caused by a virus or bacteria

The vet feeds Molly milk. The tube in Molly's neck is held in place by a bandage.

The vet puts goat's milk in a giant baby bottle. She has to hold the bottle up high for Molly.

The vet puts a little tube in Molly's neck. It doesn't hurt and is an easy way to give Molly the medicine she needs.

Soon Molly is better and back with her mom.

Molly is healthy and growing. She is almost as tall as her mother!

Wanted:
One Hairy Mom

Remy's mother got sick before he was born. She could not take care of Remy.

Orangutans need to be raised by other orangutans. Remy needed a foster mother to take care of him.

Madu is a grown-up orangutan. She never had a baby of her own.

But she had cared for two other orangutan babies that didn't have moms. Would Madu be a foster mother to Remy, too?

Wild Word

FOSTER MOTHER: An animal that is not family but cares for a young animal like a mom

Remy is an orangutan baby. Young orangutans stay with their moms for five to seven years.

Remy snuggles with Madu.

With his blanket and toys, Remy went to meet Madu. It was love at first sight. Soon Remy climbed on Madu's back.

Remy watched Madu. Madu taught Remy what to eat. She showed him how to hang and climb. Remy learned how to be an orangutan.

Toys for Tots

All babies love toys. Zookeepers try to get the right toy for each baby.

Sloth babies cling to their moms. A stuffed pillow works, too.

Even the youngest monkeys can learn to hang from ropes or chains.

Elephants love splashing and swimming in water. A kiddie pool is lots of fun!

Polar bear cubs like to chase and pounce on a ball.

A treat frozen in ice is a puzzle for curious panda cubs.

Young tigers like to play with each other. Another tiger is better than any toy.

Saving a Seal Pup

Guinness is a gray seal, just like this one.

Even ocean babies need help sometimes.

Wildlife rescuers saw a seal pup on the beach. Seals leave the water to rest. But this little guy was too thin. He didn't go back in the water. He was in trouble.

Rescuers wrapped him in a wet towel and took him to the hospital. They named him Guinness.

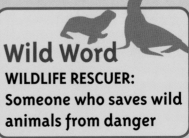

Wild Word

WILDLIFE RESCUER: Someone who saves wild animals from danger

21

Guinness had a broken jaw. The vets operated and put a wire in his jaw. The wire held the jaw together while the bone healed.

Three months later, Guinness could eat by himself again!

Guinness enjoys a frozen fish in ice—called a fishsicle.

It was time to go back to the water.
Everyone cheered when Guinness
scooted back to the ocean where
he belonged.

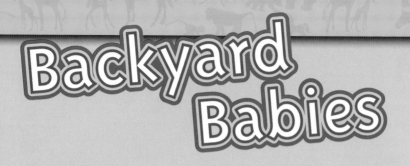

Backyard Babies

Do you want to be a vet when you grow up?

You might want to be like Dr. Greg Mertz. People know him as the Odd Pet Vet. He takes care of all kinds of animals that need help.

Dr. Mertz helps a snake.

This three-month-old goose has a broken wing. The bandage works like a cast on a broken arm.

This painted turtle has a cracked shell. The bandage keeps away infection.

People bring hurt animals to Dr. Mertz. Many wild animals get hurt on roads. Luckily, Dr. Mertz can help most of the animals he sees.

Springtime is busy for Dr. Mertz. That's when many babies are born. Animal babies like to explore. Sometimes they get into trouble and need help.

Dr. Mertz to the rescue!

These opossum babies were found in the wall of a house.

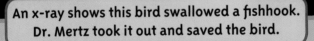

An x-ray shows this bird swallowed a fishhook. Dr. Mertz took it out and saved the bird.

Raccoon cubs can live on their own after three months. Until then, Dr. Mertz keeps this one safe.

A baby starling needs to eat every half hour around the clock!

Dos and Don'ts

What can you do to help baby animals? Here are some dos and don'ts . . .

 DO slide a ramp in a pool if you see baby frogs in it. Then they can climb out safely.

DON'T feed ducks and other birds bread. It's bad for them.

 DO wait 24 hours before rescuing a baby deer or bunny. The mother is probably nearby.

DO

tell an adult to call animal rescue if you see anyone hurting an animal.

DON'T

adopt a wild animal. They do not make good pets.

DO

prevent pets from harming wildlife. Put a bell on your cat's collar. Keep your dog on a leash.

DO

pick up trash you see in the woods. Plastic bags and bottles can hurt animals.

DON'T

pick up a baby bird that is on the ground. Ask an adult or call a vet or the local Audubon Society for advice.

Stump Your Parents

Can your parents answer these questions about baby animals? You might know more than they do!

Answers are at the bottom of page 31.

When tigers are born, they _____.

A. Drink milk
B. Are hungry for meat
C. Don't sleep
D. Sing

What do young orangutans learn from older orangutans?

A. How to find food
B. How to hang and climb
C. How to be an orangutan
D. All of the above

What should you do if you find a baby bird on the ground?

A. Run away
B. Leave it alone and tell an adult
C. Bring it home
D. Give it some candy

4

Wait 24 hours before rescuing a baby deer or bunny because _____.

A. It likes to be alone
B. It might be out getting a snack
C. The mother is probably nearby
D. It could be on its way to a party

5

Where does a seal pup live?

A. In the mountains
B. In the ocean
C. In the forest
D. In a department store

6

What do elephants love?

A. Chocolate
B. Reading
C. Water
D. Doing jumping jacks

7

What kind of milk can you feed a baby giraffe?

A. Chocolate milk
B. Goat's milk
C. Soy milk
D. Milk shakes

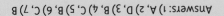
Answers: 1) A, 2) D, 3) B, 4) C, 5) B, 6) C, 7) B

EXTINCT: A group of animals that is no longer living

FOSTER MOTHER: An animal that is not family but cares for a young animal like a mom

INFECTION: A sickness caused by a virus or bacteria

LITTER: All the babies born to an animal at one time

VETERINARIAN: A doctor for animals, called vet for short

WILDLIFE RESCUER: Someone who saves wild animals from danger